# I Know That!

# Push and Pull

## Claire Llewellyn

### Photography by Ray Moller

# W

## FRANKLIN WATTS

### LONDON · SYDNEY

First published 2003 by Franklin Watts
96 Leonard Street, London EC2A 4XD

Franklin Watts Australia
45-51 Huntley Street
Alexandria, NSW 2015

Series advisor: Gill Matthews, non-fiction literacy consultant and Inset trainer
Editor: Rachel Cooke
Series design: Peter Scoulding
Designer: James Marks
Photography: Ray Moller unless otherwise credited
Acknowledgements: Davy Bold/Eye Ubiquitous: 13b.
Fred Bruemmer/Still Pictures: 20b. Angela Hampton/Ecoscene: 14r.
Thanks to our models: Chloe Chetty, Nicole Davies, Georgia Farrell,
Arden Farrow, Alex Green, Madison Hanley, Aaron Hibbert,
Chetan Johal, Kane Yoon.

A CIP catalogue record for this book is available from the British Library

ISBN: 0 7496 5165 2

Printed in Malaysia

# Contents

# Give it a push!

Pushing is a way
of moving things.

▶ *You push
a scooter.*

▲ You push a
drawer closed.

What would
happen if you
pushed this
tower?

◀ You push
a pram.

5

# Give it a pull!

Pulling is another way of moving things.

▶ *You pull a toy.*

6

How would you close the drawer again?

▲ *You pull a drawer open.*

▶ *You pull on a sock.*

7

# Get moving

Pushes and pulls are called forces. You need a force to start things moving.

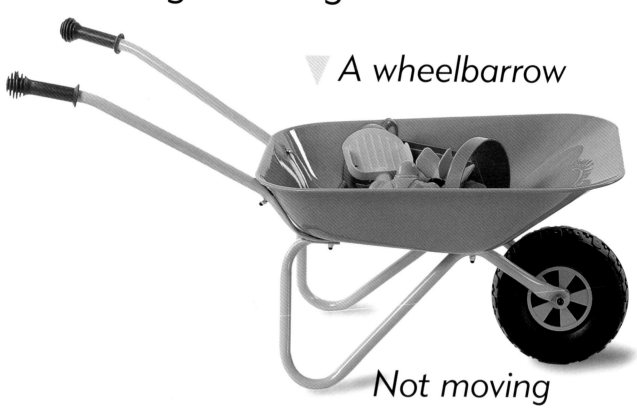

A wheelbarrow

Not moving

How would you start this bag moving?

Push!

Moving

# Little push, big push

A little push moves things just a little. A big push moves them more!

▶ *Push a toy car and it moves along the ground.*

With a friend, try pushing a car along the ground. Who can push it further?

▲ Push the car harder and it moves further.

# In the playground

The games in a playground start with a push, but they all move in different ways.

*Push! A roundabout spins round and round.*

▲ *Push! A swing moves forwards and back.*

A swing moves faster if you push it harder. You are using a greater force.

▶ *Push! A see-saw moves up and down.*

# Slowing down

A push or a pull can slow things down. It can make things stop.

▶ *Pull!*
*Make the dog walk slower.*

You could not stop a real car with your foot. It is much too heavy!

◀ *Push! Stop the car with your foot.*

# Squash and stretch

A push can squash something.

*You squash a sponge when you push it with your hand.*

What happens when you let the sponge go?

A pull can stretch something.

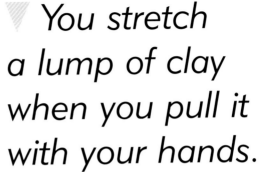 *You stretch a lump of clay when you pull it with your hands.*

What will happen if you pull the clay too much?

# This way and that!

A push or pull can make things move one way, and then another. It can make them change direction.

*Kicking pushes the ball...*

*this way...*

How can a goalkeeper
stop the ball before it
goes in the net?

*this way...*

**Goal!**

*and that way!*

# Wind and water

The world is full of forces.
Wind and water can push things.

*Wind pushes the branches on trees.*

Make some bubbles using a wand and soapy water. What happens as you blow?

◄ *Moving water pushes a wheel around.*

# I know that...

**1** You move things with a push or a pull.

**2** Pushes and pulls are called forces.

**3** A big force moves things more than a little one.

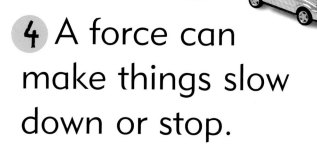

**4** A force can make things slow down or stop.

**5** A push can squash things.

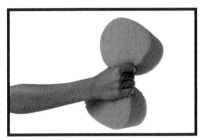

**6** A pull can stretch things.

**7** A force can make things change direction.

**8** The wind and water can push things.

# Index

## About this book

*I Know That!* is designed to introduce children to the process of gathering information and using reference books, one of the key skills needed to begin more formal learning at school. For this reason, each book's structure reflects the information books children will use later in their learning career – with key information in the main text and additional facts and ideas in the captions. The panels give an opportunity for further activities, ideas or discussions. The contents page and index are helpful reference guides.

The language is carefully chosen to be accessible to children just beginning to read. Illustrations support the text but also give information in their own right; active consideration and discussion of images is another key referencing skill. The main aim of the series is to build confidence – showing children how much they already know and giving them the ability to gather new information for themselves. With this in mind, the *I know that...* section at the end of the book is a simple way for children to revisit what they already know as well as what they have learnt from reading the book.